Satan Stalking

Dorothy Marie England

Forward Movement Publications
Cincinnati, Ohio

Cover illustration by Pete Harritos

© 1993, Forward Movement Publications
412 Sycamore Street, Cincinnati, Ohio 45202

Thanks to my adoptive parents, Bill and Ruth Evans, who knew me and loved me anyway; my husband David, who loved me before I was well and who makes my manuscripts presentable; and thanks to those who offered their support after reading the manuscript, such as David Cook, Beau Carson, Francis McNutt, David Collins, Walter Wink and John Polkinghorne.

Thanks to God who continues to save me.

Table of Contents

Prologue

Many years ago J.B. Phillips wrote a book titled *Your God is Too Small.* It has turned out that the god of rational materialism is too small, indeed. As Walter Wink states in his introduction to *Unmasking the Powers,* ". . . materialism itself is terminally ill, and let us hope, in process of replacement by a worldview capable of honoring the lasting values of modern science without succumbing to its reductionism."* Or, as John Polkinghorne expresses this thought in his work, *Science and Creation,* "The very transition from the naively objective world, as perceived by Newton and Maxwell, to the elusive quantum world of Heisenberg and Dirac is a tale of the often reluctant recognition by physicists of the strangeness of what actually is. If encounter with the physical world can so sharply revise our understanding of what can rationally be said about its nature, it would scarcely be surprising if the pursuit of the divine required openness to the unexpected."**

Trying to be sophisticated people in a rational materialistic culture, we have had to deny much of our own personal experience. I was fascinated by an experiment I recently read about. People sitting at a lunch counter were observed by a hidden TV camera. They were exposed to various "impossible" phenomena, such as the face of a demon appearing in the mirror facing them. The subjects never "saw" what they didn't believe in. They never reacted to the "impossible" stimuli.

Fortunately for our generation the box in which we tried to place God and the physical world is not only cracking, it is breaking in two with the advent of the "new" physics and the prophetic insights of theologians such as Dr. Wink.

This is especially fortunate for those of us who have experienced the reality of spiritual beings and need to tell about it. It is both comforting and thrilling to read Dr. Wink's words speaking of angels and demons: "These mighty Powers are still with us. They are not 'mere' symbols—that too is the language of the old worldview that is passing, for we now know that nothing is more powerful than a living symbol. As symbols they point to something real, something the worldview of materialism never learned to name and therefore never could confront."

But even without encouragement from such luminaries as the Drs. Polkinghorne and Wink I would have to speak. The mighty acts God has done for me are like fire in my bones. The fire smoldered for seven years as I studied, thought about and interpreted my experiences. But it had to burst free or it would have consumed me.   —D.M.E.

> *A mighty fortress is our God, a bulwark never failing; our helper he amid the flood of mortal ills prevailing: for still our ancient foe doth seek to work us woe; his craft and power are great, and, armed with cruel hate, on earth is not his equal.*
>
> —Martin Luther

———

*Unmasking the Powers, Walter Wink, Fortress Press, 1986, p.173.

**Science and Creation, John Polkinghorne, New Science Library, 1989, p.85.

But Paul knew that is was an angel of Satan—alas, it did not therefore retreat; but he knew that it was profitable to him that this happened, and hence he knew that angel of Satan was still a messenger of God. Is not this a miracle; to transform an angel of Satan into a messenger of God. Would not this make even Satan himself tired! For when the angel of darkness attires himself in all his terror, confident that, if he can only get Paul to look at him, he can petrify him with terror; when he goes on to taunt Paul that he does not even have the courage to look at him, then the apostle fixes his eyes upon him, he does not hastily shrink back in fear, he does not strike him down in terror, he does not look around with a faltering glance, but he looks firm and un-moved. The more he looks, the more clearly he perceives that it is a messenger of God who visits him, that it is a friendly spirit who wishes him well. One almost feels sympathy for the poor devil: to wish to terrify in this way, and then to stand there, his schemes understood, changed into their opposite, only concerned in getting away.

—"The Thorn in the Flesh"
Søren Kierrkegaard

Reprinted from *Edifying Discourses, IV*, by Søren Kierkegaard, translated by David F. Swenson and Lillian Marvin Swenson, Copyright © 1946 Augsburg Publishing House. Used by permission of Augsburg Fortress.

CHAPTER ONE

Childhood

This story is about evil in its many facets, as I've encountered it personally in my own life and vicariously in the lives of others. Throughout my career, I've worked in settings where the results of evil are apparent—a psychiatry department of a medical college, an urban county welfare department, a hospital for the chronically mentally ill, and in addiction counseling. I'm a recovering alcoholic and drug addict, and a child of adoption. I was oppressed by evil spirits, from which I was delivered at a Cursillo seven years ago.

C.S. Lewis said that Satan's most effective illusion lies in convincing us that he doesn't exist—that only the uneducated and unsophisticated would entertain such superstitious beliefs. This book is written for anyone who suffers as a result of evil, sharing experiences similar to mine, but, as I was, unable to place them in a proper framework and find relief. For years I denied the reality of evil. I saw psychiatrists, hoping for answers which would explain and relieve my fears. At last, admitting that what I suffered was real and couldn't be explained otherwise, I accepted the fact that an evil spirit or spirits were bothering me and began talking to my pastor. That was the beginning of recovery. When I accepted the reality of personal evil, deliverance became possible. There are many good books available concerning deliverance, but they are written by persons involved in healing ministry. This book is from the perspective of a sufferer who hopes that other sufferers will be healed.

The book is also about good—about how God always overcomes evil through love, and only through love. Good never uses the tools of evil—neither manipulation, nor lies, nor force nor fear. Good never argues, never threatens, never belittles, never accuses. Good promises abundant life, wholeness, freedom, joy, and peace of mind and soul.

†

My story starts in Tennessee. I was adopted at nine months of age and went to live with my new parents. Earlier, I had lived in the Tennessee Children's Home. My first memories are of a tiny country community called Wrigley. My dad was a blacksmith, a skilled worker, so we were relatively well off. We had electricity and indoor plumbing—luxuries there—and boasted an electric wringer washing machine, set on the front porch for passersby to see. I recall pretending to make ice cream cones out of the suds I scooped from the top of the washer. My dad was a quiet man who worked hard, went to church, and read the funnies to me every Sunday. My mom was outgoing, loved to sing, was involved in all the community activities, had many friends, and loved all creation and life in general. We had a sweetly disposed, long-haired, white dog named Beauty, and a pig, whose name I don't recall, and on whose head mom tied pink ribbons. I suspect I don't recall the name of the pig because one winter when times were hard we had the pig slaughtered for meat. Mom, of course, was against it, and predicted that it would go bad because it was wrong to kill a pet for food. The meat did spoil, but dad said it was because the butcher had poorly prepared it. My parents argued, but never fought. They were affectionate people who demonstrated love both verbally and physically.

I should have had a happy childhood, but in pictures of myself as a toddler my face has a worried look. I remember mostly fear, even of pictures in fairy tale books. My mother would try to read them to me, but I was too frightened of the pictures. I remember one warm day when there was a party outside, perhaps a birthday party. There were lots of toys and a book of fairy tales was lying open on the grass. I tried peeking at a picture, wanting so to look, but it frightened me terribly. I was also afraid of heights. My parents loved to take trips. On one of them, we went into the Smoky Mountains where mom and dad were offered an opportunity to climb up a ranger's tower on a mountaintop. I screamed in fear most of the way up the tower while they tried to console me, then became frozen with fear at the top and had to be carried down. Fear of heights rendered me terrified of bridges. When we traveled, I got down on the floor of the car if we approached a bridge, not to emerge until mother assured me we were well over it. I was afraid to be alone. As a small child, whenever left alone in a room I would be overcome by a terrible panic and would scream until someone came to me. I was afraid of the dark and had horrifying dreams. I often slept in my parents' bed. This fear was my own as a toddler; it wasn't taught to me by my parents.

After years of study of myself and others, I believe fear is the primary symptom of evil. Anger, hatred, and the misuse of money, power and sex are only expressions of fear. As a recovering alcoholic I read in Alcoholics Anonymous (AA) literature that fear is the foundation of the problems of alcoholics. I resisted this concept for a long time; now I embrace it, not only for alcoholics, but for everyone. For me, fear was the primary symptom of oppression, and as I grew older I became fearful of many things. I was afraid I wasn't pretty. I was afraid

I wouldn't be popular. I was afraid people would reject me. I was afraid I wouldn't be smart enough. I was afraid my parents would die. I was afraid I wouldn't get the things I needed or wanted. I was afraid of spiders and bugs. I continued to fear heights, the dark and solitude.

The fear of being alone involved a dread that some apparition beyond the normal would appear and I would go insane. This fear occurred especially in closed places such as rooms, elevators, etc. I never rode an elevator alone without feeling that something horrible would materialize, and missed many elevators waiting for someone to ride with. When left alone at home, I couldn't bear to stay inside, and sat on the porch until my family returned. Uncomfortable in my room alone, I constantly kept a pet with me, believing somehow even the consciousness of a dog or cat would prevent the unspeakable from materializing. I feared looking into a mirror when alone—afraid I would see something awful there—something just waiting for me to look at it reflected in the mirror. Yet I never experienced a supernatural occurrence, never saw a ghost nor a flying saucer. The supernatural experiences didn't come until later.

As an older child, I fed obsessively on ghost stories and never missed a horror film, seeing Dracula, Frankenstein's monster, the Wolf Man and the Mummy many times. I usually hid under the seat when the terrifying scenes came on. My parents had open minds about the supernatural. They hadn't seen a ghost nor had a supernatural experience, but they loved a good story. Summer nights were spent in the swing on the front porch with friends, in rockers or in straight-back cane chairs leaning against the house, telling stories of hauntings. There was a time in my childhood when my mom had a ouija board which we played for fun, and when it was my turn I always pretended to the others there was something moving the pointer. Never once did I have a paranormal experience.

However, I did have a full spiritual life. We attended a little country church my parents helped build. Circuit-riding preachers of many denominations preached on rotating Sundays. The singing was rich and wonderful. We had dinner on the grounds—picnics on blankets with fried chicken and potato salad and homemade cakes and cookies. People laughed, told stories and quoted scripture. My mother loved to sing, and the songs she knew were mostly church songs—*I'll Fly Away, Peace in the Valley, I Come to the Garden Alone,* and *He Lives.* We had a radio, and the only station we could get was in Nashville. We listened all day to wonderful gospel music, with the bass deep as the ocean floor and the tenor high as the sun. We prayed. God was as much a part of mother's daily experience as I was. And mom saw God as good. No judgmental, threatening deity for her. She loved Jesus, who didn't condemn the prostitute even though Jewish law called for her death; Jesus, who called the tax collector out of the tree to follow him; Jesus, who loved the poor and who was comfortable with leaving the rich to their own reward. Evil wasn't large in my mother's reality, and condemnation and punishment seldom came my way. Mom praised God and people, so encouragement was usually my lot.

I followed in mother's footsteps. I loved to sing and always sang in the choir. I had a rich spiritual life, talking to God throughout the day, having special God-places in the woods where I communed with him—I was never afraid in open spaces—and while other children pretended to teach school, I pretended to teach Sunday school and had a small group of children I "taught" each week.

Early childhood was blissful in many ways; I knew of nothing to fear, yet I was paralyzed by an awful fear which I couldn't articulate and couldn't explain.

CHAPTER TWO

Who Is Satan and Why Is He Interested in Me?

Sherlock Holmes, in *A Study in Scarlet,* remarks to Watson, "How often have I said to you that when you have eliminated the impossible, whatever remains, however improbable, must be the truth." Several months before I went to Cursillo I began to experience physical manifestations of evil. Unable to find other explanations for these occurrences, I became convinced of the reality of evil spirits. I will describe these experiences, but first I want to tell about what I believe Satan and his fallen angels intend, what their purpose is in bedeviling humankind.

Satan in Hebrew means "enemy" or "adversary." The Bible pictures Satan inciting God's creatures to go against God's advice, accusing those he loves of some weakness or error, lying about God's nature, and harming or destroying his creation. The evangelist John reports Jesus calling Satan a murderer and declaring him to be the father of lies. Jesus says the devil sinned from the beginning, and the reason the Son of God appeared was to destroy the works of the devil. Throughout scripture we observe Satan portrayed as God's enemy, hurting God by harming, deceiving and alienating God's people. God loves his creation and sees it all as good; Satan murders, deceives, accuses and destroys his creatures. God, all powerful, perfect and complete, can be affected only by hurting his beloved creation and interfering with his relationship with his people. Satan saddens God by convincing God's people they are worthless and lying to them about God's nature. Jesus reflects God's reaction to Satan's attacks when he weeps over Jerusalem, saying he would have enveloped her with his arms like a mother hen covers her chicks with her wings, but they would not accept him. Christ mirrors God's sorrow at the grave of Lazarus, where he weeps over illness, death and lack of faith. Satan has one goal, one plan; he is single-minded. The goal is to cause God pain any and every way he can. Satan and his evil spirits have no primary interest in me whatsoever. To them, I'm merely a means, less than nothing. Their target is God. They can only affect him because of his great love for me.

John Polkinghorne is a theoretical particle physicist, president of Queens' College, Cambridge, England, and a fellow of the Royal Society. He is also an Anglican priest. Dr. Polkinghorne, in his book *Science and Creation*, acknowledges that quantum physics allows for the existence of a noetic world, a world of mind or spirit, saying that "There might be active intelligences in that noetic world, which traditionally we would call angels. There might be powerful symbols, the 'thrones or dominions or principalities or authorities' of Pauline thought. . . .There might even, I suppose, be other entities which shared man's amphibious complementarity in the world of matter, and so were able to act within the world, but which operated, not within localized bodies, but within whatever flexibility there might be in overall process."*

In the fall, 1991, issue of *Cross Currents—Religion & Intellectual Life,* in an article titled "God's Action in the World," Dr. Polkinghorne shared his own belief that evil is allowed by God because God is love. Because of his great love, God allowed some freedom, not only for humanity, but for all creation. God is the God of life, not of mechanical automata.

*New Science Library, 1989, p. 76.

His greatest, most profound creation is a universe free to operate with some will of its own. Creation isn't programmed like a computer, allowing only preset behavior and responses. It is alive! And this life, this freedom, is the most complete expression of God's infinite love. If this is true, and I believe it is, God made his angels free to love or not, to serve or not, to be in his will or not. For there to be real freedom, there must be a real possibility of evil. With no possibility of error or wrong choice, there is, in effect, no freedom. So in his great love, God took the enormous and painful risk that his creatures would not return his love, that, instead, they might rebel, turning against each other and him. What love the Father has given to us and to all his creation!

God's love for me is absolute because he is absolute. Anything that hurts me causes him pain. When I'm unhappy, he's unhappy. I was created to enjoy God forever. Anything which interferes with that enjoyment grieves God. Whenever Satan deludes me into believing God doesn't love me, or that I can't trust him, or that he is powerless to help me, God suffers. Anytime Satan causes me to feel fear, anytime Satan causes me to be unloving, God weeps. God is and always has been Satan's target, and power over God is his aim. This is the only reason he has the slightest interest in me. But because of this, he is tirelessly and relentlessly interested in me.

CHAPTER THREE

How Satan Operates—The Accuser

Satan hurts me and the rest of creation through his three modes of operation. He is an accuser, a murderer and a liar. Scripture says he has been all three from the beginning (i.e., John 8:44ff). There has never been a time when Satan wasn't actively accusing, murdering and lying. Remember, the serpent was already in the garden.

The Biblical account of the history of God's interaction with his people begins with his creation of all things, which he then called good. Satan accuses me, not to point out my flaws to God, but to convince *me* that I'm bad, shameful and poorly constructed. Speaking to Eve in the garden, Satan accused God of not wanting humankind to share God's attributes. Our first encounter with Satan created simultaneous doubts about the goodness of God and our own worthiness. Scripture makes it clear that God in his love and goodness never wanted us to become conscious of good and evil—of the unspeakable, unfathomable difference between ourselves and him. God in his love never wanted us to comprehend the absolute differences in our natures. He hoped we would remain like little children who don't yet know that they and their mother are separate beings. Satan twisted this difference, making it appear to us that we were shameful things since we were so much less than God. Satan told us God didn't want us to share his attributes of omniscience, omnipotence and eternal life.

The truth, of course, was that there could be only one God. He knew if we discovered the awful difference between us and him, we might become resentful. Resentment is a toxin which destroys relationships. Peace and joy, which God made us to experience, are impossible in a creature alienated from its creator. God, of course, was right. As soon as our eyes were opened we became self-conscious and ashamed of ourselves. This self-consciousness in relation to God began our tragic history of fear, anger, shame and destruction. Seeing our creaturely-ness up against God's creator-ness, we hid ourselves. Even now we're still ashamed, not because of mistreatment by our parents or society, but because we know we aren't God. We won't accept ourselves as a good creation; if we can't be the creator, we refuse to be happy.

Every time Satan convinces us through his accusations that God's creation isn't good, God suffers. God loves variety and never makes the same thing twice; not even identical twins are completely alike. Satan barges into our psyche and tells us our nose or ears or feet or hands or breasts or penises are too big or too small, our hair too thin or too thick, that we are too tall or too short, that our skin is the wrong color, that freckles are ugly, that we are dumb, that we can't speak as well as others, that we are ugly, or that no one likes us.

When we believe such things, God suffers. Believing these lies, we logically conclude that God isn't good or he doesn't love us. God asks us as he asked Adam and Eve, "Who told you you are ugly, or that parts of your body are too large or small, or that there is something wrong with your color?" Satan's input is always negative—he always accuses us of being imperfect, flawed and worthless. Believing Satan's accusations, we are ashamed; shame alienates us from God, each other, the rest of creation and even ourselves. Whenever we judge any aspect of God's creation as bad, we judge God, and he is grieved.

The Pharisees had many laws concerning defilement; one was the prohibition against eating with unwashed hands. We still pursue some of these rituals because they promote good health. But the Pharisees, going beyond God's intent of promoting healthy living for his people, loaded these directives with moral content. Matthew 15:1-20 describes how Christ brought this lie of Satan to light. When he was criticized by the Pharisees for eating with unwashed hands, he let them know that nothing physical which we eat can defile us spiritually; rather, we are defiled by evil words which come from the heart. Satan tells us aspects of the created world are "bad." God made many atoms, each atom made of many subatomic particles. None of them in any of their myriad configurations are bad. Some particular combinations are unhealthy if ingested or touched, but none are morally wrong or disgusting. We may see how silly such thinking is if we try to envision a bad, revolting electron, proton or neutron!

In the garden, God asks Adam and Eve "Who told you you were naked?" God doesn't say nakedness is bad or shameful. Satan does. We continue the error of Adam, Eve and the Pharisees when we believe our bodies or any bodily function or any physical aspect of God's creation is not good. As St. Paul says, some things are not profitable for good physical or emotional health, but nothing in God's creation is bad. We don't see ourselves as being fearfully and wonderfully made. We launch our children's careers in shame when we tell them how "bad" their feces are. We use words such as "stinky" or "nasty" when we clean them, with our faces scrunched up in disgust. Children learn that they are bad, foul, revolting because what comes out of them as a natural and healthy process is declared bad, foul and revolting. We cooperate with Satan in pronouncing creation and life processes disgusting. Satan tells us because we have physical bodies with finite intellect and abilities, because we are capable of immorality and error, because we are not created equal with God, that therefore we are shameful. So we hide and cover up, believing ourselves ugly and malformed. We think God made a bad creation rather than a good one. We accuse God of being unkind, unjust, and unloving in creating such a poor work. Seeing creation as unworthy of admiration and love, we cooperate with evil by murdering ourselves, our fellow creatures and our environment.

Satan continues to accuse us day and night. There is no let-up, even in our dreams. God speaks with a "still small voice." God never intrudes. Remember that St. Paul, as Saul, witnessed Stephen's sermon and his stoning. So Saul was questioning; his mind was open when God met him on the road to Damascus. Satan always intrudes. He never knocks; unless the door is locked and barred he barges in. He seldom accuses us of present immorality for fear we may be converted and change our behavior. He always accuses us of things past, over which we may do nothing but feel shame. He brings to consciousness the ill-tempered word, the base desire or act, the alienating remark from yesterday.

He also shames us about physical attributes over which we have no control. Three voices speak in our minds; one ours, one God's, and one Satan's. We can always tell when it is Satan; Satan always accuses. If the voice in our minds says "You're stupid," "You're ugly," "No one likes you," "Nothing you do is worth anything," "No one needs you," "You never do anything right," it is always Satan. Satan accuses us of immorality or shames us over our bodies, abilities or intellect in ways which point out our powerlessness. His goal is to produce fear, dread, depression, hopelessness and shame in order to make God sad. God's voice is always bidden. Jesus says that he stands at the door and knocks. He never enters unless we open the door of our minds and invite him in. God never accuses. When the Holy Spirit provides insight into our thoughts and behavior, he also provides the power to joyfully change.

Accepting Satan's lies, we too became accusers. We constantly accuse God, others and ourselves. Most often we accuse ourselves, not of immoral behavior, but of things related to our physical or mental limitations, things we do or say which show that we aren't God, mistakes we make as a result of our limited knowledge and abilities. We feel the most shame when we make a mistake as a result of ignorance, or of a physical process or condition over which we are powerless. Curiously, we seldom feel real shame when we make a moral error such as cheating, stealing, lying, gossiping, rationalizing that everyone does "it" and we are better than most. Yet we burn with shame when we make a superficial social error or a small mistake at work or in school. We break the laws of God and humanity daily, frequently gleefully, certainly shamelessly. We drive over the speed limit, drive under the influence of alcohol and drugs, cheat on our income tax, cheat on our spouses, steal from the company ("small" items and time), lie when confronted with error, distort the reality of our worth at work or at home, kill our family, friends and acquaintances through character assassination, extinguish the light of life, freedom, creativity and love in our children, spouses and co-workers with the damper of our fear, anger and depression— and yet feel no great shame. But we feel appalling shame when it's discovered that we've made an error due to our lack of omniscience or omnipotence.

Although we don't feel great shame over our own moral indiscretions, we enjoy announcing the immoral behavior of others. Satan loves to accuse everyone of everything, and he easily enlists our aid in this because of our own feelings of unworthiness. We join Satan in accusing our family, friends and acquaintances whenever an opportunity arises. Led by Satan and our own insecurity, we devise frequent opportunities to criticize others' flaws and gossip about their sins.

Whenever I assume Satan's role as accuser of myself or others, God suffers. When I believe Satan's accusation that God's creation isn't good, God weeps.

CHAPTER FOUR

Satan Is a Murderer

The book of Genesis tells me God created the earth and everything in it, and pronounced it all good. Satan convinces me it's bad, making me unable to believe in a loving, good God. He also uses disease, destruction and death to obscure my perception of God's love. Satan kills, maims and destroys, then says, "Where is the all-loving, all-powerful, just God? You're in a world where bad things happen, terrible, awful things. Children are sexually abused, tortured and killed by their parents. Millions are starved, degraded and gassed in concentration camps. Thousands die slow, painful deaths from cancer and other chronic, progressive diseases. Earthquakes, tornados, floods, and famine destroy life and property. Where is God? Why does he allow degradation, suffering and death? God tells you to be peaceful, not anxious or afraid. He must be lying, he's not to be trusted. He's playing a cruel joke. No one cares, there is no one to help. You're on your own in a hostile universe."

God in his great love allows freedom in his universe. The holy angels were created to enjoy God forever and to participate in his servant nature by caring for humanity, just as people were created to enjoy God forever and participate in his nature by caring for the rest of finite creation. There isn't much that makes me happier than caring for another creature, whether plant or animal, a tender reflection of the joy I'm sure God experiences as my servant. But freedom allows choice, divergence from God's will and purpose. For freedom to be real, the possibility of evil must be real. When some of the angels decided to become God's enemies, they changed from caretakers to murderous destroyers. When I move out of God's will I, too, become a destroyer. Since God's will is always creating, redeeming, sustaining love, destruction is always the end result of being out of God's will. Destruction takes many forms; physical destruction and murder are only the more obvious. There is destruction of mental and physical health, destruction of trust, destruction of joy, destruction of personality, destruction of talent, destruction of hope, and destruction of love. Satan and the fallen angels feel great power when they destroy, especially when they destroy trust, hope and love in innocent beings such as children and animals. Human perpetrators also feel powerful when they destroy. Destruction and death *appear* to be the ultimate power. Satan, his angels and their human recruits leave no area of life and creation unaffected in their efforts to achieve power over God. Outside God's will, we rival unclean spirits in ruthlessness.

Human beings can be influenced to go to any lengths to destroy. Consider the serial killer, one of Satan's most treasured individuals. One person is capable of bringing terror to a community, to a state, to the whole nation. One single individual may murder in such a way that millions ask "Where is God? How could a good God allow such evil?" One person may create profound doubts on a deep, emotional level, disturb dreams and affect the peace of millions. Serial killers, usually without conscious understanding, are driven to perform atrocities which appear to prove that God is nonexistent or weak or uncaring. They prey on the weak—children, women and the chemically dependent—to foster the illusion that God can't protect them. You've never heard of a serial killer who preys on football players! Murder becomes a progressive, addictive process. As their addiction progresses, serial killers murder more and more often, performing increasingly more bizarre rituals, forcing the question: is there any evil God won't permit? If God isn't able to protect the innocent from such horror, who is safe? Such murders seem so senseless that they leave us reeling, filled with fear, wondering if the universe is crazy and if God is powerless or dead. But they aren't senseless; they produce Satan's desired effect. They bring God's power and goodness into question, and invite us to act as God's judge.

Despots serve Satan well. The genocide of the Jews, the Cambodians, the Native Americans, and the Australian Aborigines is senseless and brutal. These groups were victims of a murderous madness which possessed the minds, souls and bodies of the perpetrators. The more senseless and brutal the murders, the more powerless the victims, the more it appears that God isn't able to defend and sustain his creatures. Satan's greatest delight is in presenting God as powerless or unloving or both. Torture and spiritual, mental and physical destruction of the powerless are his most effective illusion-producing mechanisms.

Of course, it is possible to torture the powerless and innocent without murdering them, often leaving a damaged, bitter, angry, resentful, shamed, hopeless, hate-filled person to spread the word that God is powerless and unloving. As a counselor, I have met so many adults who were physically, emotionally and sexually abused as children, and who are now filled with their own proofs that God is unloving and powerless so that no ray of light can access the darkness locked in their hearts. Unknowingly they become Satan's ambassadors, telling everyone how ineffective or unconcerned God must be to allow such atrocities to occur. They mightily resist any offer of hope or love, convinced the harm done them overrides any evidence of God's mercy. Refusing to be healed, they carry the message of a weak, uncaring deity wherever they go. Having been brutalized, hated, objects of sexual perversion, they become Satan's allies demonstrating that evil overcomes good.

We who have not suffered the impact of such devastating sin also become carriers of Satan's message by discussing almost gleefully the atrocities of others. One of the most popular recent movies, *Silence of the Lambs,* won the Academy Award for best film. It's the story of a serial killer who murdered helpless young women, performing horrifying acts and even engaging in cannibalism. Another popular film, *Sleeping with the Enemy,* shows a husband physically and psychologically abusing his wife, and in the end attempting to kill her. We pay millions to see such material, and we delight in reading and telling others stories of perversion, abuse, murder or destruction, any demonstration that God is dead. The news, talk shows, soap operas, supermarket tabloids, and casual conversations proclaim this truth about our nature. The desire to hear and pass on evil information has the earmarks of addiction. People are even labeled "newsaholics," "talk show addicts," or "gossip junkies." Many of us experience feelings akin to withdrawal when we miss the news or our favorite soap operas, and we feel drawn, almost compelled to read the tabloid headlines while waiting in a grocery store checkout line. If we hear a bit of juicy gossip we can't wait to pass it along, driven almost against our will to spread proof of God's powerlessness over evil. When we enjoy seeing and discussing evil, we help develop Satan's illusion that God isn't good.

When I carry Satan's message, I participate in Satan's destructive nature. St. Paul says love covers sin. Satan wants to expose sin, and get it the widest possible audience! Satan destroys by killing reputations, murdering good names. St.

Paul says love doesn't delight in evil, but delights in good. Christ says whoever hates his brother is a murderer. When I become Satan's accomplice by uncovering the evil of friends, family, neighbors and celebrities, I tear into them so I may discount them, and when I discount them, in a significant way I kill them.

God never intended creation to suffer. Christ heals many and varied disorders whose origins he ascribes to Satan. The prophet Isaiah (11:7-9) says that on God's holy mountain the cow and the bear will eat together and the lion will eat straw; there'll be no death caused by carnivorous acts. On the Day of the Lord, "They shall not hurt or destroy in all my holy mountain; for the earth shall be full of the knowledge of the Lord as the waters cover the sea." Isaiah tells us God promises Satan won't always be allowed to cause death and destruction in his creation. A new heaven and earth will be created where there'll be no more tears, only gladness and rejoicing forever (65:17-19).

But for now, Satan has *limited* freedom to bring death and destruction, hurting God by hurting his creation. Because of the power given him to uphold creation, he was able to invade and alter the gene pools, producing carnivorous behavior, deformity and disease, and to enter into physical systems, causing destruction. Scientists studying chaotic systems—unpredictable systems which don't follow a linear pattern—have developed a new theory of chaos. This theory is based on the observation that many active physical systems, from storms to planetary orbits to the beating of human hearts, are chaotic in nature, which means that a very tiny fluctuation makes a big difference. The flutter of a butterfly's wings in Tokyo may cause storms in New York several days later. However, researchers found there is always an "attractor"—a powerful force which holds the chaotic system together while allowing for considerable freedom within the limits prescribed by the attractor's control.

In other words, complete randomness, what we previously believed chaos to be, doesn't exist in the universe. Every system which appears random is held together by a power which gives it direction and integrity. And every system which appears perfectly ordered and rhythmic carries an element of chaos—random disorder which allows for variation and change. Satan causes physical, mental and emotional disorders and destruction of land and property by effecting minute changes, injecting tiny input in genes and large physical systems. In his role as murderer, Satan convinces me that either God is powerless or he doesn't love me. When fear keeps me from enjoying a loving relationship with God, God grieves.

Because God shared the wonder and delight of his caretaking nature with much of creation, including the angels and humanity, and also shared some of his freedom, evil is both possible and real. Satan, his angels and humanity were intended to reflect God himself, participating in his joy by nurturing, building up and cherishing creation. Because of his great love, God allows freedom; he allows Satan and humankind to bring death, spiritual and emotional degradation, and destruction. But God maintains an attraction—the force of his loving will— which will never allow total destruction nor permanent death, and which will finally create a new heaven and new earth where Satan's ability to harm will be bound up forever; there will be no more tears, and life will be eternal.

CHAPTER FIVE

Satan Is a Liar

Satan enters human history in the third chapter of Genesis. His first recorded words are a lie.

He asks the woman a question, pretending he doesn't know the answer. Satan never wants humanity to comprehend the extent of his knowledge and power. He deludes us into believing we can manipulate him through magic, rituals or willpower. He wants to appear much smaller and weaker than he is, as a manageable force or entity. This is one of his most powerful deceptions! It engenders one of the two facets of codependency, a disorder in which sufferers try to manage the unmanageable in hopes of finding permanent happiness in the temporal. Satan wants us to believe we are more powerful than evil. He tells us the only reason the world isn't perfect is that we haven't worked hard enough to make it so. This is a primary fallacy of humanism. Satan wants us to believe we can make things good if we exert enough willpower. He enjoys this deception so much that he doesn't at all mind appearing less than he really is. Deceived, we keep our eyes on ourselves and our own resources, rather than looking to God to redeem and sustain us. Believing we can somehow manipulate our environment in a way which will eliminate evil, we fail to see that ultimately only God has the power to overcome it.

Continuing in this vein of pretending diminished capacity, Satan's most successful deception is his disappearing act. C. S. Lewis points this out in his book, *The Screwtape Letters*: "My dear Wormwood, I wonder you should ask me whether it is essential to keep the patient in ignorance of your own existence. That question, at least for the present phase of the struggle, has been answered for us by the most High Command. Our policy, for the moment, is to conceal ourselves." Satan leaves us groping, trying to discover the source of the world's evil like children in a game of blind man's bluff. We blame addiction and crime on poverty and neglect, yet both middle-income and privileged persons become addicts and criminals. Crimes committed by differing socioeconomic groups fall in different categories, but they are still crimes! We say sexual abuse is the product of poverty and ignorance, but those who work with abuse know it is an equal-opportunity disorder, just as are other manifestations of addiction. We like to think that ignorance is a function of poverty, but as a mom with a child in a private school attended by those much wealthier that she, I know this is one of Satan's lies. We want to believe that violence is a product of the hopelessness of the ghetto, but violence occurs in the "best" of families.

By pretending to be weak or non-existent, Satan fools us twice! First, believing that evil has only a human source, we believe it is humanly manageable. Second, seeing that we haven't managed it, we believe we and our neighbors are to blame. In *The Magnificent Defeat,* Frederich Buechner says, "Call it what you will, the evil in this world is greater than the sum of all human evil, which is great enough, just as the evil in ourselves is greater than the evil we choose, and that is great enough too." Satan has injected evil into the very fabric of the created universe; physics' second law of thermodynamics tells us every system goes from order to disorder; energy is continually dissipated. But there is a dark meanness which transcends universal decay and disorder, overpowering and dampening any unaided creature's struggle toward truth and light. Martin Luther says in his great song, "A Mighty Fortress," "for still our ancient foe doth seek to work us woe; his craft and power are great, and armed with cruel hate, on earth is not his equal." St. Paul says we don't struggle with flesh and blood, but with principalities and powers (angels and other supernatural beings), and in this struggle we need the whole armor of God. David sings "[God] is my refuge and my strength" (Psalm 71:7). But Satan continues to pretend weakness or non-existence, the latter supposedly confirmed by 19th century western scientists. Many 20th century scientists who have explored the quantum world, relativity, chaos and the fine-tuned universe are more open to spiritual possibilities. Not willing to believe in higher spiritual powers, I tilted at windmills and struggled with smoke, blaming myself and my fellows for not overcoming the evil in the world, filled with anger and fear.

Satan's second sentence is a lie about God. He says God is a liar.

Satan pretends to be less than he is, lulling us into believing we are the stronger; but he presents God as less powerful than evil. Satan offers us a topsy-turvy view of reality, in which we are more powerful than he, but he is more powerful than God! This leaves us to imply that since we are more powerful than both God and Satan, we can be our own god—The Great Lie.

Eve is told that if she eats the fruit of the tree she will not die, a lie which, in effect, makes her more powerful than God. The logic goes like this: God says if I eat the fruit I will die, but I won't die; since God lied and I know it, I'm more powerful than God. This is a lie which all addicted people believe, that they can practice their addiction with no harmful consequences. Addicted people laugh at those who follow God's advice about the practice of monetary, chemical, sexual and culinary temperance to maintain physical and emotional well-being. Then, believing Satan's lie, they feel put out—unjustly dealt with—when visited with the inevitable consequences of behavior God warns us against. Those of us who are addicted ingest all sorts of poisonous chemicals, engage in promiscuous sexual behavior, indulge in chronic anger and resentment, overspend our resources and whine that it is unfair when our bodies, emotions, minds and souls perish. Believing Satan's lie that there won't be consequences, we blame God and others for our failures and sicknesses and despair when we become ill or rejected or arrested or divorced or fired or bankrupt or insane.

Satan convinces us God is lying by misrepresenting his motives. In the Garden, Satan tells Eve that God doesn't want her and Adam to eat the fruit because if they do they will become like him. In other words, God is jealous of his position. This lie presents an invitation to experience terrible misery. If we believe it, we see our humanity as a shameful thing since we aren't equal with God, affording Satan enormous opportunity to function in his accusatory mode. A tiny little *whissssper*— four little words implying that we weren't like God, that "God is a liar"—changed history and brought the most profound suffering for billions of people.

Second, the lie implied that God doesn't want the best for us, making him out to be the enemy of his own creation! This is the kind of twisted-all-the-way-around-backwards thinking involved in all evil premises. One of the manifestations of Satanic possession presented in *The Exorcist* was the victim's head turning around backwards. In a black mass, the Lord's Prayer is said backwards. Evil is always 180 degrees wrong, while Satan's powerful lie makes it look perfectly right. Satan uses all his wiles to convince humanity this premise is true, that God doesn't wish the best for his people. Presenting God as unloving is evil's greatest delight.

Third, Satan's lie implies that knowledge will not only provide us with a very limited share in one of God's attributes; it hints that through knowledge we can become God. Human history is primarily a record of our struggle to control ourselves, our fellows, our environment and creation itself. God controls through attraction; remember the chaos model. Only God's saints can control through attraction; the rest of us attempt to control through power. Killing appears to represent the ultimate in control. So the knowledge we apply in attempting to control ourselves and our environment often ultimately leads to death—death through diminishing resources, death through pollution, death through extinction, death through despair—all in the name of progress, the mistaken belief that knowledge will make us God.

Satan lies to us concerning God's nature. He convinces us that God isn't just and loving, that at best God is indifferent and is often unjust, unloving and cruel. This lie grieves God more than any other, since it distorts his very essence, separating him from his beloved creation. Satan says that since "bad things happen to 'good' people," God is bad or weak. And God's very loving nature prevents him from directly discrediting this deception.

An awful paradox develops here; the supreme Love which allows freedom appears as indifference or unjust cruelty when twisted through the prism of Satan's lie. Satan accuses Job of loving God only because of all the good things he has given him. In other words, God bought him off! Satan says, "Job loves you because you never allow anything bad to happen to him—you manipulate him into loving you by giving him good health, great wealth and a wonderful family. If you let bad things happen to him he won't love you anymore" (Job 1:9-11). So God, in his great love for Job, allows him to be free to love, not because of health and wealth, but because of the transcendent, ultimate and eternal relationship with himself. Fueled by Satan's lies, outward appearances show an uncaring or mean God who brings destruction to his servant. Satan's witnesses taunt Job, telling him he must have sinned in order for God to be punishing him so. Job knows he did not sin in the usual sense; therefore the only conclusion must be that God has unjustly withdrawn his love. Job is bitter, complaining that death is preferable to life, that it would have been better if he hadn't been conceived or had been left alone as an infant to die! Now bereft of all temporal benefits and pleasures, Job can respond freely when God presents himself. There is no longer any suggestion that Job's response is a hope or expectation of earthly gain. Job's response to God's presence is awe and love, based not on what God has given or may give him, but on what God *Is*. Job really sees God for the first time, and he falls in love.

In this profound, wonderful story, Job sees and falls in love with God's reality. Sadly, all stories don't have such a happy ending. In spite of his suffering, Job kept questioning. He kept an open mind so that he stayed receptive to God's presence. Usually, our minds snap shut at the first sign of adversity, leaving us believing Satan's lie that God is unjust and unloving.

Satan always lies. Sometimes he lies outright, but usually his lies are more subtle. He tells half or three quarters or even ninety-nine one-hundredths of the truth; but always leaves out or distorts the most important piece, turning the whole concept upside down. He quotes scripture out of context. He makes what is bad appear good, what is wrong appear right, what is foolish seem smart or debonair. Christ calls Satan the father of lies, saying the truth is not in him (John 8:44). If any situation causes confusion, if anything is a lie, there should never be any doubt as to its origin. And whenever we embrace anything short of the truth, we become Satan's children. Lies generate doubt and misunderstanding, the perfect climate for the production of Satan's most cherished emotion—fear.

CHAPTER SIX

Devils' Food

"Your adversary the devil prowls around like a roaring lion, seeking someone to devour" (1 Peter 5:8).

All of God's children must eat. David speaks of the Israelites in the wilderness eating the food of angels. God feeds people and angels with spiritual food. Christ says people don't live by bread alone, but by every word that God speaks. Unclean spirits, rejecting and refusing spiritual food, are continuously and ravenously hungry.

Christ says those who hunger and thirst after righteousness are blessed because they will be filled. Evil spirits hunger and thirst after unrighteousness, death, destruction and fear; and like addicts, they never get enough!

People and angels were designed to live on God's Word—the body and blood of Christ—love, peace, creativity and freedom. This spiritual food is anathema to the fallen angels. Their delicacy is fear.

Peace is an overriding theme in scripture. When an angel appears to a person, its first words are "don't be afraid." Again and again Christ tells his hearers not to be anxious about anything. The apostles preach peace—the peace of God that passes understanding. When Peter talks of Satan as a roaring lion, seeking someone to devour, it's in the context of overcoming fear and anxiety through trust in Christ. The holy angels, Christ, and the apostles, preach peace because fear is food for devils. Where there is no fear, evil can't flourish. When peace abounds, Satan finds no nourishment.

The original "Star Trek" television series developed this concept in an episode in which an alien being who fed on negative emotions invaded the ship. The crew began to fight among themselves, verbally at first, then physical fights broke out. Quickly, everyone was angry at everyone else. Resentments frothed, bubbled and boiled. Finally, Mr. Spock, the First Officer, free from such human feelings because of his Vulcan nature, identified the conflict's source. With strenuous effort he then convinced the others that the alien had planted paranoid ideas in their minds to produce food for itself—fear, anger and violent, negative emotions. Once the crew realized they had been deluded, they were able to stop the assaults and rekindle friendly feelings for each other. Deprived and starving, the alien left the ship.

Evil spirits behave similarly. They attack on all fronts—physical, spiritual and psychological—to produce feelings of depression, hopelessness, fear, anger and resentment—devils' food. When the attack is productive they stay and feed. Finding a fertile field, they continue the attack, engendering more and more negativity. The more they eat, the more they want, never satisfied, never filled. Fear is multiplied by fear. Hate develops into murder. Perversions become more and more twisted. Just as in people, the addictive process in evil spirits is progressive. The more they eat, the hungrier they become! And like addicts, they will go to any lengths to get the sustenance they crave. Like great, obese horned worms they munch on fear, chew on anger, chomp on perversions, and gobble up gossip!

While their delicacy is fear, their staple is unrighteousness, anti-love. Day and night, awake and in our dreams, we provide food for the devils. Any unloving thought nourishes them. The hatred, violence, murder, lust, and envy we conceive in our hearts nourishes them. They feed not only on unloving actions, but on every report of an unloving thought or act.

St. Paul said that love hides sin. Expounding this theme in his book, *Works of Love*, Kierkegaard shows how uncovering and talking about sin multiplies it. If I talk about my neighbor's sin, I multiply sin in the world! If I read a book about sin in order to savor it, I multiply sin. If I enjoy a movie or watch a television program which degrades creation and depicts the destruction of innocence or peace or joy, I multiply sin. Whenever I read or hear about another's fallenness, smacking my lips over their degradation, rolling their misery around on my tongue, evil grows. One sin in a human heart sprouts and multiplies like a grain of wheat, then passes from mouth to mouth, like a terrible parody of the the body and blood of Christ, providing food for Satan and his hosts. However and whenever I participate in unrighteousness—anti-love—I spread a table for my enemies.

Fear Blossoms and Brings Forth Fruit

It's said that we often outgrow childhood's fears. This wasn't true in my case. As I grew into womanhood, all my fears and phobias increased. I was what others call painfully shy, which meant I was terrified of people and had no idea what to say to them. If I spoke, the wrong words often came out, leaving me red with embarrassment. I was fearful of the opposite sex since I believed that at best I was unattractive. Yet I yearned to have friends, girlfriends and boyfriends. I began a desperate study of popular people, trying to imitate them in order to be at least marginally accepted.

My fear of bugs continued to grow. Arachnids frightened me particularly. A small spider would keep me out of a room. As an adult, fearfully cringing outside the door I would send my children in to destroy the enemy. Afraid as I was, I was even more afraid of dispatching the offensive creature myself.

Fear of heights almost disabled me. I couldn't go up over three floors in a building. Fortunately, I lived and worked in situations which usually didn't require me to go any higher. But on the occasions when it was necessary, I would stand for long periods before the elevator, paralyzed with fear, trying to find courage to ascend. If I managed to get on the elevator—never alone, always with others—and go up, I would be unable to tolerate the height, develop vertigo, and have to come directly down! I limited my travel to highways and areas where I wouldn't have to cross over high bridges. One year I traveled with my mother and two small daughters to New York City, planning the route so that mother would drive over the George Washington Bridge. Mom took the kids up in the Empire State Building, but just looking up at the skyscrapers made me dizzy. Fear of heights meant fear of flying, but my job required me to fly several times a year. Having learned to use alcohol to mask fear, I would arrive early at the airport to drink as much as possible before boarding. I even carried alcohol in my flight case so I would always have it available. Yet I never approached intoxication on flights; fear produced adrenaline so that it canceled out much of the alcohol's effects.

I grew even more afraid of being alone in a closed-in space. Most fearful people lock themselves inside houses or rooms. I was more afraid if doors were closed or locked! I would open every door and window if I had to be inside alone. Frequently I would sit on the porch waiting for someone else to come home rather than being alone inside. The enemy I feared wasn't human, not someone who would enter from the outside to attack me. The enemy seemed to hover around me, with the greatest danger of its becoming manifest when I was inside, alone. I still expected a demon to appear.

I continued to fear mirrors for the same reason. Unlike Dracula, who couldn't be seen in a mirror, the demons I feared might appear if I looked in the glass. This fear was compounded in a double reflection; my room had a little dressing table with a triple mirror into which I compulsively avoided looking. I felt that evil entities were always near, just waiting for an opportunity to gleefully manifest themselves if I became alone in a room or looked into a reflective surface. Consciously, I tried to deny the source of my fear. Intellectually, I didn't "believe" in the supernatural in the form of real demons or Satan as a real spiritual entity. But the repression was shallow and if I looked into my mind and heart I could glimpse the source of my fear hiding only slightly beneath the surface. This split in my understanding of reality affirmed my fears concerning insanity.

Of course, the content of my intellectual food kept fear fat. At that time, I didn't understand that spiritual food impacts the soul and psyche just as physical food impacts bodily health. "You are what you eat" embraces the spiritual and intellectual realm as well as the physical. I continued to read books and see movies whose themes were the horrible and the bizarre. When the old Frankenstein, Mummy, Dracula and Wolf Man movies went out of vogue, I graduated to science fiction, the paranormal, and contemporary, more sophisticated horror—Ambrose Bierce, Shirley Jackson, and ultimately Stephen King were among my favorites. I remained ambiguous about this fare. Part of me hungered for it. I would longingly search the library and book stores for a new book. Once I had it, I would read it as one who was ravenous would eat a scrumptious meal, unable to stop until it was finished. Yet there was a part of me which loathed it, hating to look at the words or scenes, feeling dirty, afraid and remorseful afterwards, like a sex addict after an indulgence. But that part of me which was driven to it was stronger, and I spent much of my extra money and leisure time pursuing a world in which God was powerless and the strange and terrible were the norm.

Nightmares graduated into night terrors. I would lie para-lyzed in bed, beaten and tormented by evil forces. I literally felt my body tugged and pummeled. Unable to scream, I would have the sensation of dying. Once awake, I would feel sore and expect to find bruises from the beatings, but none were ever visible. The nightmares also continued and grew more bizarre. One night I was in an eerily lighted woods, surrounded by cavorting woodland creatures and demons; I was hanging on a white cross. In another, little devils were chasing creatures across a strange landscape as I tried, fruitlessly I knew, to hide. These dreams were the kind in which you can't tell if you're awake or asleep. Thirty years old, divorced and living with my parents, I would crawl trembling into their bed after a night terror or nightmare. I learned that increasing doses of alcohol would put me to sleep, but by around 3 a.m. the effects would begin to wear off and the horror would begin.

I'm not alcoholic because of my fear; I was born with genes which predisposed me for the disease of chemical dependency. But fear exacerbated the disorder and prevented recovery. I saw psychiatrists, but like most alcoholics I was never able to be absolutely honest with them. I never told the whole truth about my drinking and I never divulged the demonic basis of my fear. I was afraid they might think I was crazy. With a sincere desire to help, they gave me minor tranquilizers—Valium, Atavan and Xanax—then antidepressants and sleeping pills. Although over the years I remarried and got a job as a chemical dependency counselor, by 1983 alcoholism completely disabled me. My husband was caring and astute enough to force me into treatment, where he insisted I stay in spite of my pitiful pleas to leave.

A dear friend and supervisor helped me keep my job, so upon leaving treatment, I entered AA and returned to work. The old fears continued, but free of mind-altering, mood-changing chemicals, I began to have new experiences. While awake and without warning horrible scenes of carnage would appear in my mind. I would see cut and bleeding, dismembered and mangled bodies. I would be driving down the street or counseling with a patient when suddenly the awful picture would flash behind my eyes. Sometimes I knew the victim and sometimes not. Often it would be a family member. But either way, the scene was startling, terrible and terrifying.

Physical manifestations began and were equally without warning. I would be singing my little daughter her goodnight song when I would be startled by the glimpse of a disturbance in the air, almost imperceptible, perhaps a disturbance in dimensional space in another part of the room. What I saw wasn't corporeal in the usual sense and is difficult to describe, but I saw a presence and knew it wasn't benign. I think Martin Luther saw such a presence and threw an ink well at it! This presence would surprise me at almost any activity, either when alone or in the company of others, at any time of the day or night except when asleep; then the nightmares or night terrors might start.

Other physical manifestations occurred. On one occasion, while cooking breakfast before dawn, I heard a loud racket in a little entrance room at the back door. It sounded as if a large object were crashing about, bouncing off the walls and among the articles stored there, knocking them down and breaking them. Opening the door to see what in the world had happened, I found nothing disturbed. On another occasion, I came home from work to find that a large, very heavy plant container full of dirt and plants had been turned completely upside down on its stand on our deck. The house was locked and the deck and pool were enclosed with a seven-foot fence whose gate was locked. No one could have had access to the deck, and I couldn't imagine any animal or other disturbance which could have turned over so exactly such a large, heavy, cumbersome object.

All my life I had tried to believe my fears were a product of my own psychology rather than being based in any sort of reality. Now reluctantly I admitted that reality embraced more possibilities than my narrow philosophy had allowed.

I went to see my pastor.

CHAPTER EIGHT

Living Water

Although young, the assistant pastor of the large, historic church I attended in Augusta, Georgia, seemed to have an honest spirituality which made him wise. When I told him in detail my history and what I believed to be happening—that I was being attacked by one or more evil spirits—he didn't respond with disbelief. He took my complaint seriously, but since the study of deliverance from evil spirits hadn't been included in his training and wasn't a normal church activity, we were at a loss as to how to proceed. Yet his ministry to me was precious. He gave me the affirmation I needed, not discounting my experiences or attributing them to hysteria or hallucination. Without his encouragement, I might never have found the courage to ask for deliverance when an opportunity did come.

I hadn't been totally without spiritual experiences. As a young woman in 1962, I saw Christ. It was just before an evening church service. The church was almost empty. I was under considerable stress; I was going through a divorce, had a poorly paying job, little education and two small children to support. I was feeling terribly guilty. Kneeling in prayer, I looked up at the pulpit and saw Jesus standing there. I saw him in a spiritual body rather than a physical one; his form and features were indistinct. But I knew it was him because he said, "Come on, it's all right." I felt his love, and knew he wasn't interested in the great sins I had committed. He was inviting me to enjoy a friendship where he would protect me and make me well—like a mother hen drawing an injured chick under her wing. I cried for several hours, so glad he loved and accepted me in spite of my mistakes. But Satan quickly diverted me, and this encounter with Christ didn't develop into a real relationship until many years later.

In 1983, I was bringing our four-year-old daughter home from a birthday party. It was before noon, but I had already been drinking brandy. At this point in my illness, just prior to treatment, I was taking morning drinks to relieve the shakes and treat other withdrawal symptoms. My little girl was fastened into the back seat by her safety belt. Hearing a sound behind me, I looked back at her, turning the wheel too far to the right and heading off the road. Seeing what I did, I corrected too much, and ran off the road on the left. Traveling at 35-40 miles an hour, we plunged down an incline of about 30 feet and into a heavily wooded area beside a stream. I was completely unable to maneuver the car by then; we were out of control. Our daughter said she saw me shifting gears and turning the wheel. I have no memory of anything between going over the edge and resting safely at the bottom. We hit nothing! The car was a total loss, its frame bent from stress. I had a small crack in a vertebra and our child had a bruise on her side from the seat belt. As Sherlock Holmes said, having eliminated the impossible explanation that somehow I had driven the car, I knew God must have intervened to save us. My angel took over and drove for me, I'm convinced. I entered residential treatment for alcoholism a few weeks later.

Although I spent a month in treatment and was attending AA, my recovery from chemical dependency hadn't yet begun. Believing myself to be bright and spiritual, I didn't bother to work the steps of AA or get a sponsor. In reality, I was still unwilling to turn my life and will over to God. I still wanted to do things my way even though my way had brought nothing but misery. After six months' abstinence, I drank again, not daily as before, but episodically on random weekends. This was, perhaps, the hardest period in my illness, neither comfortable in my misery as an active drinker nor really in recovery. In retrospect, I believe I would never have recovered had I not attended Cursillo and experienced deliverance there.

The next year, we were invited to go to the Diocese of Upper South Carolina's Cursillo 28. I was afraid and angry, and didn't want to go. My husband, a state prison chaplain, wanted to bring the KAIROS program, a program similar to Cursillo, into the prison. He had to experience a Cursillo in order to do this. Several people from a Christian community in Augusta who were heavily involved in both Cursillo and KAIROS sponsored us to go. I was afraid of these people, and had paranoid ideas concerning their intentions. I expected Cursillo to be some weird, cultish experience. Dragging myself along only because my husband said his work required it, on a chilly November night I found myself outdoors at a church camp in the deep woods, shivering with cold, fear and alcohol withdrawal, silently going through the Stations of the Cross!

In case some reader hasn't yet been to Cursillo, I won't tell enough to spoil the surprises it holds. But I will say that Cursillo provided a succession of the most wonderful and powerful spiritual experiences I've had, and this would have been true even without deliverance! On one of the days in this four-day weekend there was a healing service. At this service, God performed a mighty act for me.

I didn't believe much in healing. I thought there was something hysterical about those who sought it, and something which smacked of the charlatan in those who were practitioners. In spite of my experiences, I was still holding on to rationalism, not believing God could or would intervene in the natural process. We attended the service. Those who were willing to ask for healing formed lines in front of our spiritual advisors, three priests—two men and one woman. Each petitioner would tell the priest about his or her illness, then kneel to receive a prayer and a blessing. The rest of us who didn't need a physician were standing around the perimeter, watching and supposedly praying. Suddenly I realized I was seeing God.

The whole large room appeared to be under shimmering water. Light danced everywhere—in the air, over the walls and around the people. The light was alive, covering everything and everyone—bright living water. I thought, "God is here. I should ask for healing." I wanted to get in the woman priest's line, but it was too long. So I got in the shortest line, because I wanted to be healed fast! The priest leaned close, and I whispered the nature of my illness: "I need to be delivered from an evil spirit, or some evil spirits." He didn't seem shocked. I knelt in front of him and he held my hand with one hand, and put the other on my head.

I was knocked down with a delightful force, like electric butterflies coursing all through my body. I couldn't move, overwhelmed by the powerful and wonderful feeling. I was being cleaned from the inside, head to toe. The beautiful, dancing, living water washed every cell, and I was filled with light.

CHAPTER NINE

God Finishes What He Starts

St. Paul promises that God finishes what he starts (Philippians 1:6). For me, the deliverance at Cursillo was a beginning. I soon discovered I had been healed in many ways. My phobias were gone. I was no longer terrified of heights or bugs or spiders, and I wasn't afraid to be alone. For the first time in memory I wasn't driven by fear. Anger—fear dressed up to appear scary, like the Wizard in "The Wizard of OZ"—subsided. I rarely had a night terror or nightmare. Obsessive thoughts no longer chased their tails through my mind. I not only lost interest in supernatural books and films, I felt a revulsion just entering an area in a book store or movie rental business where they were displayed. Even my handwriting changed. Previously I had tended to write with a downwards slant; now my writing was much straighter across the page.

I was having a wonderful time. I rode elevators alone, up to the top floor of the tallest buildings I could find. The military hospital where I worked had 13 floors, and I gleefully rode up and down. I would almost embrace any bugs or spiders I saw, delighting in the wonder of their appearance. I spent as much time alone as I could muster with a husband, a job and a five-year-old child. I went to church, to AA, and praised God much of the time.

But I found I wasn't completely well. I still had an occasional night terror or nightmare, and continued to have rare visions of the torn, mangled body of a family member appear in my mind. I was still occasionally drinking.

My husband, my daughter and I took our annual Christmas trip to the beach less than two months after Cursillo. I drank during this vacation. Sometime in the night on New Year's Eve, I had a nightmare or hallucination, I don't know which, of Satan dragging me down a non-existent drain in the middle of the floor in the bathroom. The next morning, I decided enough was enough. As soon as we returned home, I asked an AA friend to be my sponsor. This wise person insisted that I go to "step meetings," meetings in which AA's twelve steps are discussed. I began an honest attempt to work the steps, and have continued to live by them. I haven't drunk since. But even without alcohol, the nightmares, night terrors and visions continued. I knew that a spirit or spirits had returned.

A few months later at noon on Ash Wednesday, I was in church, once more almost alone, awaiting the service. I was praying and crying, asking God to deliver me from evil. Suddenly, God was there. I didn't see him visually this time, and wasn't knocked over by the delightful power of his Spirit. Instead, I felt a glow starting in the center of my body and moving out. I felt my face burning; it felt as if it were shining. I kept my head down as much as possible during the service, afraid the heat I felt radiating from my face might be visible. The glow continued as I drove back to work. I went quickly to my office, still fearful that someone would see my face shining. I called my husband to ask him what might produce this feeling. He reminded me of the *shekinah*—the glow on Moses' face after seeing God. The glow I experienced was pale in comparison with that of Moses, I'm sure, but I felt I could have been found easily in the dark!

The visions stopped completely, and only very rarely do I have a night terror. Also, there was a quietness inside my head, a silence I had never known before. I realized then there had always been a sound similar to radio static located in the left side of my brain, just back of my ear. For the first time, my mind could be completely still. Peace of mind was what I had desperately sought—through relationships, jobs, alcohol and tranquilizers—and finally I had it, through a mighty act of God.

CHAPTER TEN

Hugs and Kisses

My priest tells a story of how he was sitting in a hospital waiting room with his head in his hand, anguishing over the illness of a friend, when he felt an arm go around his shoulders. Thinking it was another friend there who had come up, he turned to speak to him. No one was there. He believes it was Jesus who gave him a hug. I've never felt a physical hug, but I've experienced many of what I call "kisses." I want to tell you about just a few of them.

The Easter after my second deliverance on Ash Wednesday, we were once again at the beach; I was sober this time. When we went into the little church on the island and knelt to pray before the service began, suddenly and unexpectedly God's Spirit entered me just as it had at Cursillo. I lost my breath and leaned against the pew in front of me. Once again, I saw God's Holy Spirit dancing throughout the church like sparkling rain.

Another Easter morning before dawn, we were again at the shore, all sleeping soundly. A thought woke me up, telling me to get dressed and go out on the beach. I tried to ignore it; we were planning to get up early *enough* to go to the island church service. But the thought persisted, and I couldn't get back to sleep. Although it was still dark, I got up, dressed, and walked down to the beach. Further down the shoreline, I could dimly see the shape of a large cross and several people milling about.

As I approached, I realized it was a sunrise Easter service on the beach.

Several years later, I wrote a little book called *12 Steps to Loving Yourself*. From childhood, I had always wanted to write, but was never able to finish anything. God's mighty act gave me the freedom necessary to create something of value. I unsuccessfully approached several publishers in an attempt to give the manuscript birth. Finally, I got a call from Forward Movement Publications; they wanted to publish the book. The confirmation letter arrived on November 9, my birthday. The book was quickly published, and my first copies arrived on February 14, Valentine's Day.

My Friend and Father loves me and wants me to know it. He delights in showing his love, and he loves to surprise me with a "kiss."

CHAPTER ELEVEN

Nothing Can Separate Us From The Love of God

Persons with whom I've talked who have been involved in a deliverance ministry say it's possible for evil spirits to be passed from generation to generation. I don't know how I came by mine, but I believe they've been part of my experience from early childhood. I think evil comes uninvited if we aren't protected, as St. Paul says, with the whole armor of God. If any group feared God, the Jews certainly did. Yet Jesus found a multitude of his chosen people harassed and possessed by Satanic forces. We're told that some of them were children. The Gospel according to Mark, the shortest and earliest Gospel, refers ten times to the casting out of unclean spirits.

Jesus encountered sufferers wherever he went. I doubt that evil spirits are less numerous or active today, but because our western culture was deluded by rationalism (an irrational philosophy which disregarded thousands of years of human experience), we are unable to accurately diagnose the condition and seek appropriate help. The physical and spiritual worlds are intermingled—apparently they've never been wholly separate. Christ is eternal; always he anticipated his physical existence. In Christ God sustains creation (Hebrews 1:3), and without Christ creation would cease to exist. Kierkegaard posits that we all *know* God, we all *know* we possess an eternal soul, we all *know* the law of love. It's all part of our personal spiritual experience, but we expend much of our time and effort trying to disregard or deny what we already know! Dr. Polkinghorne speaks of our amphibious nature—we partake simultaneously of both the physical and spiritual. He believes this natural process may also work in reverse; the spiritual contains within itself and can manifest the physical. In fact, we have metaphors for this duality in the physical world itself; energy and mass are different expressions of the same reality; $E=MC^2$. Light has a dual nature—it can be wave and particle.

Evil is an expression of the freedom God gave creation out of his great love. Paradoxically, whenever we experience evil, if we understand it rightly, what we see is remarkable evidence of God's love. But another experience of God's love, which we often overlook, is the fact that evil in the world is rare compared to the good. Disorder is uncommon compared to order. Error is a small percentage in life's statistics. I recently heard someone on PBS radio say that only when the plane crashes, the hurricane or flood comes, the serial murderer is revealed, do we understand and appreciate life's order and goodness. Only when the phone rings and we hear news of the accident, only when the doctor tells us the awful diagnosis, only when the regular, ordinary goodness of life is interrupted with terrible news do we appreciate how wonderful the ordinary is. If we disregard Love, there's no reason the crash, the death, the devastating storm, the tragic error shouldn't be the norm. Scott Peck says in *The Road Less Traveled* that it isn't evil which surprises him, rather it's the fact that there is so much good.

Speaking through Isaiah, God tells us he didn't create chaos (carrying the old meaning of a series of completely random events); he created a habitable universe (Isaiah 45:18). Through the cross, Satan hoped to make God angry enough to lose himself, abandon his own nature. On Good Friday, Satan did his worst, carried to completion his most destructive plan, in hopes that he would finally overcome good, that he would cause humanity to perform an evil so horrible that it would separate creation forever from God's love. For two days God was silent. On the third day, Love overcame ignorance and fear and injustice and betrayal and cruelty and torture and death. The Great Attractor always keeps evil from ultimately overcoming good. Nothing can separate me from the love of God, nothing in heaven or on the earth or under the earth. Love prevails because love endures—God is Love. The devil gets a few hits, makes a few bases, but the final score is always God 1, Satan 0.

After healing, I discovered that all the guilty thoughts, all the accusations which had chased one after the other endlessly through my mind like a terrible merry-go-round, had come from the devil. God never accuses. Love covers the multitude of sins. Love builds up, edifies. God separates me from my sin farther than the east is separated from the west. He covers my guilt with love deeper than the ocean. Christ showed his great love for me when he took human form and suffered a horrible, agonizing death on the cross in order for me to be reconciled. He says to me as he said to the woman taken in sin, "I do not accuse you," and he adds, "and I'll suffer and die to prove it." Because he is Love, he is patient and kind, he doesn't rejoice in the wrong but in the right.

Love loves variety. He loves noses, penises, hips and breasts both great and small. He wants tall people, short people and all heights in between. He likes two sexes to complement and enjoy each other. He loves a variety of colors in skies, plants, feathers, fur and skin. He loves for some to be bright, some strong, some artistic, some scientific, some creative, some methodical, some skillful, some athletic, some studious, some generous, some frugal, some wealthy, some healthy so each may share her/his gifts with others. He created a variety of spiritual gifts for the same reason. God rejoices in the different. He never makes exactly the same thing twice. And he counts the hairs, the feathers, the petals, the cells, the molecules, the atoms, the quarks in everything he makes, loving the sparrows, loving the lilies, loving me.

The Holy Spirit heals me and builds me up. He fills me with himself, and teaches me. God's Spirit heals me both physically and emotionally. And when, because of his commitment to allow some freedom in his creation, he doesn't heal me, he turns my suffering into my good. His Holy Spirit always builds me up. He always encourages me. He shows me the beauty in myself and creation. He teaches me to delight in himself and everything he made. In his love he provides me with a mind to wonder, think and study. He created in me the ability to read and write and understand. He gives me strength to work and play. His Spirit constantly sustains me, holds together the atoms of my body and the being of my life. He gives me time. If he forgot me for even an instant, I would cease to be. But God promises never to forget me. He says that even if a mother could forget the child she bore, he will not forget me.

Love is personal. Only love is personal. Anti-love—also called evil or self-interest—is always impersonal. Self-interest is never love. Self-interest can't be personal. Anti-love always has an ulterior motive, which could be satisfied by anyone with similar qualifications. Satan and his legions don't care about me personally; they only use me to hurt God. Whenever I enter a relationship with you to meet my own needs, you are probably interchangeable with at least several others with similar characteristics. If a husband wants a wife to fight with, almost anyone willing to fight or submit will do. If a wife wants a husband to support her, almost anyone with a satisfactory income will do. Needing someone to support me in my addictive disease, I can easily find someone else if my present support tires of the role. If I'm a single parent and want someone to help with the children, anyone willing and able will do. If I want someone to listen to my sad story and support my point of view, a number of people will fill the bill. If evil assaults me, rapes me, tortures me, or even murders me, it's never personal. Even though my assailant may curse me and call my name, it's never personal. Only love is personal. Love doesn't need its object, so it's always personal. Confident that it has or will get everything it needs, when love engages in a relationship it's always to delight in the other as an individual. Love enjoys differences of appearance and opinion. Love doesn't want anything except to share some of its abundance, its joy with the beloved.

To God, it's as if I were his only child. If there had been only me, Christ would have died for me. Because he is Love, he gives me eternal life. He'll follow me anywhere, from earth to hell to heaven, pursuing me with love. And in the end, he'll create a new heaven and a new earth, so I'll never cry again and nothing will ever hurt me anymore. Because he is Love, love will prevail. Because he is Love, love never ends.

CHAPTER TWELVE

I Am...The Truth

Confused by Satan's illusions, my life had been filled with fear. By the time I went into residential treatment for alcoholism, I was afraid to go outside, afraid to answer the phone, and afraid to read the mail. I didn't have the typical uniform of alcoholic women, a chenille bathrobe, but I did have an old, stained terry cloth coverup which I wore day and night, never leaving the house. I was afraid of everyone and everything. I was afraid to sleep and afraid to wake up. I was afraid I wouldn't be able to get enough alcohol. I was afraid I would die.

After recovery and deliverance, I began to see that everything I feared was an illusion. As an only and adopted child I had always feared the death of my parents. Yet when they died, God gave me everything I needed. My mother's illness brought me a wonderful demonstration of how God's sustaining love overcomes Satan's worst efforts. Mom suffered from Altzheimer's disease the last three years of her life. First slowly, then rapidly her mind deteriorated and her personality changed. She had been bright and friendly; a happy person who loved and trusted God. The disease produced anger, fear and confusion. She cursed those she used to love and now didn't know. Before her final hospitalization, I gave her a Mother's Day present. She didn't know how to open it or what it was. She didn't know who or where she was, didn't remember how to eat, or what clothes were for. She entered the hospital on the Fourth of July, and quickly went into a coma. While she was in the coma I visited her each day on my lunch hour, standing beside her bed, talking to her about the family, about what we all were doing. One day I was talking about our two-year-old daughter, who had been her delight. Her beautiful green eyes which had been dull with disease suddenly lit up. She looked around the room, expecting to see the little girl there somewhere. I quickly told her the child was home, and she would see her as soon as she came home from the hospital. The life in her lovely eyes was soon gone, and mercifully she died a few days later. But now I understand that souls don't get Altzheimer's. Souls aren't hurt by devastating mental and physical disorders. Souls stay bright and alive and happy. Mamma had suffered physically and mentally, losing both her mind and her personality, but her soul was fine. Satan got a hit, he made a couple of bases, but he didn't score. His illusion of destruction was pretty realistic, pretty impressive. But I saw the truth: God doesn't let any of his little ones slip through his fingers.

Pain, disease, insanity, death, and destruction are part of reality, but they are temporary. Satan does his best to convince us they are the ultimate reality. Alcoholics have lots of car wrecks, and I had my share. On one occasion early in my disease, I left home to pick up one of my daughters. I was sober at the time. Looking both ways and seeing nothing, I pulled out into a seven-lane highway. Just as I pulled out, I saw a car coming toward me at a great rate of speed. I was certain it would hit me. The next thing I knew, my car was stopped on the other side of the highway, facing the direction I had planned to go. Amazed and relieved, I said to myself, "Thank God he didn't hit me." But he had hit me. He had totaled my beautiful new Mustang. The police asked me to sit in the patrol car while they worked at the site of the wreck, just to be sure I was OK and didn't need an ambulance. I was shocked and angry, but otherwise I felt fine. It wasn't until several hours later that my ribs started to hurt; the x-rays showed three were broken.

Since the wreck, and unrelated to it, I've had several surgeries—two of them abdominal, one of them the old gall bladder surgery, in which you are cut stem to stern. Imagine what happens in such an operation. A physician takes a sharp knife and makes a long, curved cut, going deep through the muscles and the abdominal wall. The gall bladder rests far behind and up under the liver. I won't go into further detail, but you get the picture. These operations were painful. Recovery was very painful, but not nearly as torturous as appearance might suggest. The pain wasn't unbearable. And every day it got better. Amazingly, the first day after the gall bladder surgery I was directed to get up and walk!

Satan always lies. The picture we get in our mind of such a wreck, such a wound, make the events seem much worse than they actually are. As with my mother's disease, God gives grace in every situation so that our soul is sustained and we never suffer more than we can bear. The illness, the accident, the surgery appear ghastly to an observer, but God provides grace for the victim, so that we aren't even aware that the violence has occurred until we have had time to begin our recovery. God absorbs some of the pain, so our suffering isn't what it appears to be. Satan blows everything up, exaggerates everything to frighten us, like a rooster who puffs up his neck feathers to appear bigger than he is.

So many times in life the thing I feared most happened, the thing about which I thought, "Oh, if that happens, I'll die." Not only did I not die, but often that very thing turned out to be profoundly good for me. I dreaded my parents' death, but I realize now that I would never have recovered if they had continued to take care of me. I would never have matured if they had lived on. I would never have wholly turned to God as long as I could rely on them. I feared poverty, but became poor and discovered I didn't need the things I thought I couldn't live without. Like St. Paul in Kierrkegaard's "A Thorn in the Flesh,"

I began to see Satan's messengers as angels of light! They showed me the truth that nothing in creation could separate me from the love of God! No matter how awful a thing appeared, God's grace cushioned me. He provided everything my children and I really needed. As a practicing alcoholic I appeared to be in full cooperation with Satan, set on bringing about my physical, mental, emotional and spiritual destruction. Family and the few friends I had left wouldn't have bet a dime on my recovery, and neither would I. But God's love prevailed. His grace and mercy sustained me and saved me. Christ was working everything out for my good while everyone, including myself, thought I didn't have a prayer!

Reality is the kingdom of Heaven. Christ is Truth, and living in Christ is living in the kingdom. Not only is Christ Truth, Christ always tells me the truth. When he says that God loves the birds and loves me even more, he tells the truth. Christ doesn't deny that birds fall, but his description indicates that they fall into the Father's hands, and so do I.

Satan makes my sin look terrible, too terrible to be forgiven. Satan tells me God can't forget my sin, that the things I've done are too shameful to be forgiven and forgotten by God, others or myself. Christ is Truth. He asked his Father to forgive those who crucified him, explaining that they didn't know what they were doing. After the resurrection, he didn't accuse the disciples of disloyalty—there is no indication he remembered it. God tells the truth when he says he refuses to remember my sins. In fact, forgiveness and remembrance are antithetical. Just think about it—suppose God said "I'll forgive this, but won't forget it," as the vicar did in *Pride and Prejudice*. Intuitively we know this makes no sense. What's truly forgiven must also be forgotten. There's a joke I love about a man who was in direct relationship and converse with God. A skeptic challenged him, saying, "If you talk to God, ask him what I confessed to him last night," knowing that only God knew what his confession was. The saint replied, "He says he doesn't remember."

Satan says, "What you've done is too bad to be forgiven." But Love covers the multitude of sins. Are you an ax murderer? Love covers the multitude of sins. Are you a child molester? Love covers the multitude of sins. Are you commandant of a concentration camp? Love covers the multitude of sins. Love bears all things, believes all things, hopes all things, endures all things; love never ends. Christ is Truth, and the truth is that nothing can separate me from the love of God.

Satan makes sin, death, disease and destruction look serious. God says nothing can separate me from his love; not anything on or under the earth or in heaven! If absolutely nothing can separate me from his love, nothing is serious! The cross says nothing Satan will ever do can separate me from God's love. The cross was the culmination of Satan's worst efforts; sin overcame perfect innocence and goodness, evil took Love and slapped it, spit on it, mocked it, disrobed it, tortured it and killed it. But Christ rose up with love intact. Christ is the Truth. And the truth is that love will always, eternally overcome evil. The truth is that nothing—not sin, not disease, not destruction, not death—nothing can ever separate me from the love of God.

CHAPTER THIRTEEN

I Am...The Life

In the last stages of my illness, death would have been welcome. The worst thing I had to face was another day; trying to get enough alcohol to hang on, making crazed phone calls in the middle of the night while in a blackout and not knowing the next day whom I had called or what I had said, suffering uncontrollable tremors and insomnia, not able to care for my family, not able to work, unable to eat. I had lost 30 pounds and had liver disease. I couldn't comprehend much of what I read. I couldn't think or remember.

Physically, mentally, emotionally and spiritually I was dying. I was an amateur scientist, a rationalist. Not believing in miracles, I was hopeless. Yet, perhaps since there was no hope it was worth a chance to ask God for help. I knelt in my kitchen, and humbly asked God to help me. Apparently that was all he was waiting for. Once I became willing, even a little, to turn my life over to God's care, he went to work. Spiritual, mental, emotional and physical recovery have been a process. The wonderful people at AA and Cursillo, my family, the Bible and AA literature—they all taught and continue to teach me. Once I opened my mind, the Holy Spirit showed me things I had never seen. Words I had read or heard before revealed their meaning. I had been seeing everything upside down, in reverse! I had thought the church said that if I had enough faith, God would do what I wanted. In reality what was taught was that to be happy I needed to conform my will to that of the all powerful, all knowing God who loves me. As the program of Alcoholics Anonymous teaches, true freedom and happiness come from doing what I ought to do because I *want* to do it! Memory slowly improved. Physical health returned. I became emotionally stable, not depressed or angry or carried away by erratic emotional reactions to every event, word or gesture as before. God healed my spirit with his presence, kisses and constant, affirming, edifying, nourishing love.

Creator, Redeemer, Sustainer; all these roles of God mean life for me. And God promises he will never change; his nature never varies, so he will always be Creator, Redeemer and Sustainer. Satan perverts, twists and tries to destroy creation. He never makes something new. God always and continually creates. Creation is his job; it's what he does. Everything that is not God is creation, and all creation is continually growing, developing, evolving and changing. Time is, as Dante pictured the universe, like a rose opening its petals. Nothing in creation ever stays the same. Nothing is ever exactly repeated. Not a petal on a flower, not a grain of pollen, not a person, not a face, not a voice, not a gait, not a fingerprint, not a cell is ever duplicated. God makes everything new. God continues to create me. One of my favorite songs goes, "He's still working on me, to make me what I ought to be. It took him just a day to make the moon and stars, the Earth and sun and Jupiter and Mars. How loving and patient he must be; 'cause he's still working on me."

Satan continuously, hopelessly and futilely attempts to degrade and destroy creation. But God is the Redeemer. He never lets his children slip through his fingers permanently. I was angry because I wasn't God. I resented God's having made me. I resented being a finite, limited creature rather than the eternal, omniscient, omnipotent God. I resented God's allowing evil to exist, and so cooperated with Satan. I agreed with his accusations that I was no good, a shameful thing because I wasn't God. Buying Satan's lie that God was weak or unloving, I set myself up as God's judge, although a more ridiculous posture is unimaginable. But God is the Redeemer. All those years, he never forgot me. And when I was ready, he showed himself to me in his power and love. There can be only one God. Since he couldn't make me God, he became human to reconcile me to him. He both enjoyed life and suffered just as I did. He sang and danced and ate and drank good wine at weddings. He was hot and sweaty, tired and hungry, tempted by Satan, abused and misunderstood, hated and plotted against by his enemies, betrayed and abandoned by his friends, tortured and killed. He lived in time like me where one minute follows another, sometimes filled with joyful anticipation, sometimes with terrible dread. He sweated blood. God wouldn't take back the freedom he gave creation because he is Love. So he entered creation and subjected himself to the freedom, the evil. And he was free. He chose. And he always chose love. He chose to enter Jerusalem. He chose to stay in the garden and be arrested. He chose not to answer Pilate. He chose to die. And it was all for me.

God sustains me. Christ promised he would live in me, giving me abundant life now and eternal happiness. Christ in me gives me time to plant a garden, grow a lily and see its bloom open with crinkled gold on the rim of the petals, deep violet changing to pale violet as the petal goes inward, bright gold sunbursts at the petal's base, and a diadem of pure white-and-gold tipped stamens. Christ in me gives me time to work at a job I love and do well. Christ in me gives me time to walk with my husband on the winding road around the river, talking about the day and our lives.

Christ in me gives me time to play with my daughter and grandchildren. Christ in me gives me time to exercise and sun-bathe and travel to exciting places like New York and Washington and Portland and Memphis. Christ in me gives me time to shop. Christ in me gives me time to enjoy my friends. Christ in me gives me time to pray for my enemies and praise him. Because Christ lives in me I have time for everything, I have both now and eternity.

This developing relationship with God brings me continuous delightful surprises. Things I once thought ugly now appear in their beauty. There is a song titled, "I've Got My Father's Eyes." To me, this means seeing creation the way God sees it, seeing everything working together for good. My nose no longer looks too long or my hair too fine. My freckles don't look ugly: as the saying goes, "A girl without freckles is like a night without stars." But girls without freckles are lovely too, and so are small noses and all sizes in between. Steve Brown of Key Life Ministries recently told the story of the caterpillar who looked at a butterfly and said, "You'll never get me up in one of those things." Satan's illusion makes us think that our present form and spiritual condition are the whole story. I want to see us from God's perspective. I want to see myself and others fully, as we really are, resurrected and alive in Christ. God's Spirit living in me gives me the ability, when I want it, to see creation through his eyes.

CHAPTER FOURTEEN

Staying Well: Progress, Not Perfection

Only three things were required to begin healing: admission of the problem, giving up resentments, and humbly asking God to deliver me from evil.

Deliverance is a wonderful, delightful and amazing voyage of discovery; I chart new territory in my understanding of God, myself, and creation. Any day may bring a bright insight or a new perspective on some beautiful, fascinating element of creation. But it is also an Odyssey of danger; a trip home filled with Sirens and Cyclopses.

Satan reads, even quotes scripture, so he knows that ultimately we're not his; we belong to Christ. But his demons still stalk every move, feeling and thought. Remember, the devil's desire to hurt isn't focused on us, but on God. So, although we grow stronger, our will is still vulnerable. He continues to enter our thoughts, twist our motives, attack our emotions and assault our bodies. God allows Satan always to have a witness, so we can always have a choice. Christ says to resist the devil and he will run away. But like Odysseus with Circe, the problem is wanting to resist. Willingness is the key which frees us from Satanic attack; the struggle lies in developing and sustaining this willingness.

Experience has shown me many of the ways in which I used to, and occasionally still do, embrace Satan. Whenever I multiply sin through gossip, I embrace Satan. When I voyeuristically read or watch sordid or scandalous or violent or degrading material, I embrace Satan. When I mentally call anyone stupid or ugly or anything less than a creature of God, I embrace Satan. I embrace Satan when I'm impatient, when I'm irritable, when I'm depressed and when I'm angry. Christ tells us to love our neighbors just as we love ourselves. Which of us wants our own sins or errors uncovered, or wishes to be thought of as unattractive or mentally deficient? Biblically we're told that love is patient and kind, not irritable. We're told to rejoice always, and that human anger doesn't work the righteousness of God. Yet I'm excited by gossip and like to see and hear about awful things others have done. Prurient interest compels me to read the headlines in the supermarket tabloids. Although I may successfully resist, I still feel drawn toward films and books like *Silence of the Lambs*. Part of me still delights in the evil rather than the good. I enjoy calling poor drivers idiots. I feel powerful when I'm angry, and sometimes I don't feel like rejoicing.

Like St. Paul, I do what I don't want to, and I don't do what I want to do. Even when it comes to physical well-being, my will isn't always directed toward health. Although through God's grace I've quit drinking alcohol and smoking, I still overeat sugar, complex carbohydrates and fat. I suffer from arthritis and degenerative joint disease, and am unable to ask for healing with a pure heart. Something in me takes a perverted delight in pain and the slight deformity in my fingers. Like a child showing off a sore, I frequently tell others about my arthritis, secretly enjoying my little participation in perpetuating the illusion that God isn't wholly good or not fully sovereign. My will hasn't entirely conformed to God's will for me, and Satan discovers and develops any opportunity.

We are or become what we see, read and think. Presently a cognitive theory of depression is making the psychological circuit. Research shows that those who complain of depression will pick out wrong or unpleasant things in any picture shown them, while those who don't suffer from symptoms of depression will see pleasant or cheerful things in the same picture. This bit of psychology was recognized by St. Paul almost 2,000 years ago as he admonished the Philippians to think about things which were true or honest or just or pure or lovely or of good report or virtuous or praiseworthy. Staying well means asking God to give me grace to see beyond and through Satan's illusions, revealing the good, the true and the beautiful in creation. It means not seeing myself and others only as we are now, growing in grace yet still ill and evil, but as we will be when God grows us into the full stature of Christ. Staying well means giving up our addiction to offensive talk shows, gossip, and degrading, frightening books and movies. Staying well means meditating on the wonder and delight in the smallest and simplest flower as well as the most complicated and precious person. Staying well means reading material which praises God and glorifies creation.

Staying well means not taking anything in creation too seriously, remembering that nothing in the created world, nothing in or under or above the earth, not powers nor principalities, not dominions nor thrones, not life nor death, nothing at all in creation can ever separate me from the love of God. Therefore nothing is serious, since the only thing that would be serious would be something that could separate me from God's love.

Staying well means recognizing that only love is personal. If a spouse betrays, if parents abuse, if friends deceive, it isn't personal. Every evil thing is done out of a sense of need. Husbands feel wives don't meet their needs and vice versa. Abusive parents feel great anger and anxiety rising which only finds release in acts of abuse. Friends deceive in order to meet some perceived need. When someone violates or persecutes or deceives me to meet a need, it is never personal. Even if they call my name when they curse me, even if they say I'm the only one who could affect them this way, need is never personal. Need often needs a scapegoat, someone to blame. If I am the scapegoat, the abuse may seem personal indeed, since the abuser treats everyone else well. But let me leave or die, and someone else, even one of the formerly favored ones, will soon take my place. Almost anyone will do. Spouses and children and friends are interchangeable scapegoats, and often are used up and exchanged. Love never acts out of need, never fears that needs won't be met. That love is synonymous with need is one of Satan's most productive lies, one more example of how the devil turns everything around backwards and upside down. Love never needs; service to God is perfect freedom. Need enslaves, love frees. Only God is always absolutely personal because he is absolute Love.

Staying well means being willing to love my enemies and to be like Christ, as harmless as a dove. Resentment was the sin of the older brother in the story of the prodigal son; he was angry at his father for forgiving the errant brother and holding a feast for him. Resentment kept him from going to the party, and resentment keeps us out of the kingdom of God. Resentful people don't want to go to heaven; it will be filled with the people they hate.

The program of Alcoholics Anonymous taught me to ask God for grace to let go of resentments; they are deadly for alcoholics. I find the same recommendation in deliverance literature. Satan and his demons feed on resentment; they flourish in its presence. Resentment is a sickness in itself, producing depression, insomnia, and physical complaints. It sours every relationship. The ultimate target of resentment is always God, who made or allowed the object of resentment to exist. Those who spread resentment abroad are propagandists for Satan's lie that God is either an unloving or inept creator. When we nurture resentment, we act as God's judge. We cherish our resentments because they justify our belief that our judgment is better than God's! Christ and AA admonish us to pray for our enemies; when we become willing to do so, both resentment and Satan lose their power. Staying well means allowing Christ to be the judge, understanding that his judgment is mercy.

As soon as I formulate my own plan and rely on the illusion that I possess my own resources, Satan seizes his opportunity. Staying well means praying only for God's will to be done and the grace to carry out my part in it. It means keeping my mind open, resorting neither to formulas for knowing God's will nor rituals to get my way. Both scripture and my own experience show me that God heals or delivers when and how he wills. He may either use a mediator or heal directly. He doesn't need certain words said in a certain way. He doesn't respond to magic! He is alive and free. He does what he wants with his own, and he always works everything out for the good of those who love him. Staying well means responding to a living Person, who is active in a creation he has endued with freedom.

Staying well means keeping company with others who are recovering from bondage, demonic harassment, or the disease of chemical dependency, whether in church or 12-step meetings. I need the sacraments, I need to hear God's Word proclaimed, I need the fellowship of grateful saints, and need the insights of others around the tables of 12-step meetings. Satan's tricks are too subtle, his attraction too powerful for me to continue my progress toward the kingdom on my own. I often hear the Siren's cry, but I'm tied to the mast of the church. On my own I would be lost.

Staying well means proclaiming the good news. As AA says, if I don't give my joy away, I can't keep it. When I fell in love, I wanted to tell everyone; I wanted to stop strangers in the street to tell them. And I must tell about God's love for me, how he resurrected me from physical, mental, emotional and spiritual death. I believe my resurrection was more of a mighty act than the resurrection of Lazarus, since it included deliverance from evil spirits. It was more of a mighty act than stopping the storm or parting the waters, since it meant curbing my desire to drink. God had to deal with two powerful and perverted wills, mine and Satan's, and I didn't even believe he could do it. I still cry when I think about it. Behold what manner of love the Father has given unto us. It's like fire, shut up in my bones. Not talking about it would be like a lover having to keep secret the fact that she has a beloved. God's grace is so wonderful and delightful that if I didn't talk about it, the rocks and stones themselves would start to sing.

Staying well means guarding my feelings. Satan and his crew feed on negative emotions. Wherever there is depression, anger, strife or fear, Satan and his band of unholy angels set up housekeeping. Feelings are nothing but the chemistry I generate dependent on my perceptions. If I see the world as a dangerous, bad place where I must fight or be abused, I generate the chemistry of fear. If I see the world as fallen but redeemed, I generate the chemistry of peace and serenity. If I see the world as an evil and disordered place where it is my lone responsibility to make things orderly and right, like Elijah, I become tired and depressed. If I see God as the all-powerful, all-loving sovereign creator, redeemer, sustainer and friend, I generate feelings of freedom, joy, security and love. Emotionally, what I see is what I get. So, like the lyrics of Johnny Cash's old song, "I keep my eyes wide open all the time." I keep a close watch on this heart of mine. Because I choose my point of view which drives my feelings I can see the world as damned or redeemed. I can see it through Christ's eyes or through Satan's. It's my choice, my call.

Seeing the world through Christ's eyes means seeing it not only as it is, dying and ugly, living and lovely; but also as it will be, resurrected as Isaiah describes. A world where the blind will see and the deaf will hear, where the lame will leap like harts and the dumb will sing for joy, where water will break out in the wilderness and streams will flow through the desert, a world where the redeemed and ransomed of the Lord will sing with everlasting joy and gladness, where the mountains and the hills will sing, and the trees will clap their hands. The Lord will create new heavens and a new earth; and the former things will not be remembered or come to mind. His people will be the offspring of the blessedness of the Lord, and their children with them. God says before we call he will answer; while we are still speaking he will respond. The wolf and the lamb will feed together, the lion will eat straw like the ox; and dust shall be the serpent's food. There will be no pain or destruction in all his holy mountain.

Sure in the knowledge that Christ was and is and is to come, and that nothing and no one can snatch me from his hand, I have faith, hope and love. I can love my natural family, my spiritual family, my neighbor and my enemy. Perfect love casts out fear, the environment in which Satan thrives. Staying well means staying immersed in the love of God, which brings the peace of God that passes worldly understanding.

> *The soul that to Jesus hath fled for repose,*
> *I will not, I will not desert to its foes;*
> *that soul, though all hell shall endeavor to shake,*
> *I'll never, no, never, no, never forsake.*
> —John Rippon's Selection, 1787

Epilogue

So after all is said and done, by Satan, by humanity, and finally by God, we comprehend the truth. The longer we look at Satan and his angels the more we perceive them as messengers of God. They show us that God loved creation so much he blessed it with freedom, the awesome freedom to make the wrong decision, even to hate and destroy. And when God allows them to destroy our work, our relationships, even our bodies as he did with Job, Satan acts as God's messenger by stripping us of earthly pursuits, comforts and dependencies so we can see God himself—his power, majesty and love transcending all worldly attachments. As Kierkegaard says, "One almost feels sympathy for the poor devil; to wish to terrify in this way, and then to stand there, his schemes understood, changed into their opposite, only concerned in getting away."

About the Author

Dorothy Marie England is a pseudonym used in deference to AA's tradition of anonymity at the level of the press. Ms. England is a Certified Addiction Counselor who has been practicing her profession 15 years. Presently she is Director of Alcohol and Drug Programs for a Regional Mental Health Center and is co-investigator into the etiology of chemical dependency with professional staff at a major university. She has written several articles on the subject which were published in national professional journals. A recovering alcoholic and drug addict, Ms. England is married to a clinical chaplain, who has served congregations, mental hospitals and large state prisons in the Southeast for 35 years. She is a mother and grandmother. Her *12 Steps to Loving Yourself* is a Forward Movement publication.